ISBN 978-1-365-26789-5
www.facebook.com/1SoulP

This was my process, and it was difficult.
Trusting was difficult.

Recorded Entries:

9/27/15	5
10/19/15	6
10/26/15	8
10/28/15	9
10/30/15	10
11/19/15	11
11/30/15	13
12/4/15	14
12/18/15	15
1/10/16	16
1/28/16	17
1/28/16	18
2/1/16	19
2/27/16	20
3/15/16	21
3/25/16	22
3/27/16	24
4/2/16	25
4/3/16	26
4/3/16	28
4/4/16	30
4/5/16	31
4/12/16	32
4/14/16	33
4/16/16	34
4/19/16	35
7/6/16	36

9/27/15

The Cape or The Retreat or Cabin On The Shore

It's peaceful here.
Waves ripple rhythmically to the beat of the current.
At their peak, colonies of bubbles shed their white shade cascading
over one another,
sounding off their crash onto the shore.
The waves aren't always polite,
but the shore is unconditionally welcoming.
It receives all the gifts the waves have to offer.

Trust The Process

1. When the day looks impossible,
   the couch feels comfortable, and sunrays splashing from the
   bay windows look uneventful.
   Trust the process.
2. When a conversation with your partner seems daunting and
   your feelings eat away at your tongues ability to produce
   words.
   Trust the process.
3. When depression is the dust that refuses to be swept from the
   floor and all you want is freedom from having to clean up the
   destructive thoughts that fall.
   Trust the process.
4. When song doesn't sound as beautiful
   and melody no longer scales your arms with goosebumps.
   Trust the process.
5. When fear resembles the worn notebook in your book bag,
   the rarely opened Evernote app on your phone,
   or the twice folded post-it notes dusting your desk that stare,
   and stare, and hover, and wait, and tire, and toggle and get
   misplaced, and are found, and still not touched.
   Trust the process.
6. You are tired and the couch is still warm from the imprint of
   your back.
   The outside taunts you to smile in its direction.
   Close your beautiful eyes and feel the heat wash your tired
   away.
7. Your feelings matter and your words hold value, use them.
   It is impossible for your partner to know the lining of your
   mind or heart or hurt.
8. When the dust settles you will still be a person. All pumping
   blood, moving limbs, and processing mind. Press your
   quaking hand against the valley of your chest,

the home where your survival lives,
the carrier of your liberation.

9. Sound waves need not an ear to be heard nor a piece of skin
   to scare. Listen to the silence of your beautiful body and
   welcome the music in your story.

10. Trust the process of your healing.
    Trust the process of your hope.
    Trust the process of your deliverance.
    Trust the process of your mindfulness.
    Trust the process of your pen.

What is Art?

Art is equal parts life and death
Dreams and nightmare
Water and rock.
It is the way things are
Should be, and
Happen to be.
Art is the biological composition of a plant
The texture of carpet, and
Taste of spit after playing the saxophone.

Look in my eyes

See me now,
in this moment.
Unfiltered and raw,
tainted by wind and life,
take me in.
Hate to love me,
I am sorry.

Post-it Note Thoughts

What my words don't show, my actions should.
What my actions don't say, my love could.
If you told me today my future could change
I'd probably toss that advice away,
Sit back, give myself a scratch and call it a day.
If being alone were as difficult as being together
I wouldn't know what's better,
Me or her.

Hey

Hey you, yes
you with the poem.
You're much stronger than the wind you
able-soul, yes
you have defeated the odds.
They stare at your back with arms wide and lonely,
hurt by your resilience.

You, yes
you with the baggage.
All you need is a carry on,
there is no more room for the sorry's of your mistakes.
They are plenty; they fueled your fury and sharpened your fight,
you don't need them anymore.

You, yes
you with the shattered love.
There is no logic to shitty people,
only hope filled goodbyes.
Hope for their consciousness,
hope they will forgive themselves for the damages they've done,
hope no one again becomes their savior.
It was a tough role for you once and you wouldn't wish that on
anyone.

Your love is not broken,
it has infinite sunrises and countless moons
left in its story.
You are the writer of the poem.
Your paperback cover has been folded, kicked, and stepped on.
Your pen is not empty,
your pencils do not dull.
Your pages are ready to be written again.

Jamaican Rum Cream

The stars are visible here,
there are no distractions,
they illuminate the deep dark sky.
The moon rests against the clouds
snoring,
counting sheep
shining authentically.
Waves clash with rocks,
it's as if their nightly argument is a series
of reruns that never get old.
You walk with me
brave
overcoming your fear of the dark,
letting me love you.

12/4/15

Journal Entry:

Everyone was asking if I was going to "pop the question" while in Jamaica. My reply was always a big no, as if I would never consider it, or consider her. I started to think about it more, felt a little bad for my reaction to people. I love her, she's incredible, everything I've needed from a partner for a long time; I want to make sure that's a step I'm ready for. I hate the constant second-guessing of my mind throughout this relationship. It's scary to grow so close to someone that they make you want to go buy a ring and see what they say. I'm so used to things not working out at this point, but I don't want to bring the past into the present. This relationship will take time, and effort, and trust, and love, and work; that's what I'll do.

12/18/15
Letter to my Journal

Don't lose faith in me,
I haven't forgotten about you.
You've been faithful and I've fallen short
too many times to count.
I haven't elapsed the color of your cover
or the smooth of your pages.
I'm surprised you remember the scent of my hands,
the utensils I use to wet your lines.
I used to think we would always have tomorrow,
that next time was around the corner.
But you are cut tree,
flammable and easily thrown away.
I, am flesh and bone and fading memory,
too afraid of making my truths real,
and not willing to give up hope that you'll
be around to listen.

1/10/16
It's Okay

It's okay to love,
take a pause on everything
you've learned, and listen
in the midst of skepticism.

It's okay to love.
To allow the
warmth that surrounds
your heart because
of it's increase in blood
circulation vibrantly pumping
through your body,
naturally reacting to
seeing that persons smile.

It's okay to smile back
the authentic you.
The one that prays at night
to meet that person you've
dreamt about endlessly.
Your pillow knows your pain,
rocks you to sleep
hoping to resign at
any moment to that
person in your dreams.
It's okay to dream.

1/28/16

To the brothers, friends, colleagues, men I've never met before, this is our problem. It is on us to talk to one another about, to urge that language and behaviors change, to listen to the countless stories of women who encounter danger in the image of us everyday. This is a narrative we are responsible for, a tragic one, one we are privileged to not have to think about as much. Whether it be attacks on bodies of women or men, we need to impact the behaviors of perpetrators. That happens when we call out and shut down problematic language and actions. They are often repeat offenders, ones who disguise themselves as everyday people. This is terrorism, this is hate crime, this is sexism, this is murder, this needs to stop.

1/28/16
**"Yet another women has been killed for turning down a man
who asked her out"**

after connections.mic

It's hard to look at the tears on my partners face
from knowing her Woman is in danger by my Man.
That my Man is capable of such gore,
and that her Woman is not safe,
even in her own Constitution
Or Being
Or Desire to be left alone.

This Mans difficulty with seeing her pain is nothing
to the rabid river her tears flood south,
over the waterfall of her cheeks
blanketing the cavern of her daily trauma.

This is the mutilation my Man achieves.
I must sit with that.

Pillowed Thoughts

The night sky and your dreams of me
hold my eye lids hostage.
They keep me up with questions like:

When did you know?
and How did you think it would happen?

The night sky and your dreams have conversations about life,
try to decipher if love is a genetic trait placed in bodies to give them
purpose for living,
Or
if it's a battle-royale of human emotion.

I didn't have answers,
only interest in how they knew our past.
Ghosts who decided to stay in limbo to share their love story with
the me insane enough to fall.
They know about living more than I do,
they found purpose in guiding crumbled faith beyond the cliffs of
terror.

Fearless

You have a flame burning blue
at the basement of your gut.
It sways back and forth
meditating
preparing
building with energy for its release.
Your eyes are gaskets to your desires;
necessities for better living.
Your dreams borderline as nightmares
for fear of their existence.
Do not fright the lever of your jaw.
Release the scorch in your belly;
barge through the habitual fables
that your teeth use to hold you back.
Lean in to the power of your potential,
be a flamethrower of a body.

On Lazy Days

There's a comfort I find in my apartment.
The angle at which my couch occupies space;
The position the TV, movie case, and end table
stare at me sedentary against the swede;
How the coffee table divides our existence;
How light clumsily splashes across my living room from the bay
windows;
How the pictures, eye sockets to the walls, know more about me than
myself;
Know how my habits inform my decisions;
Know the intersection of my depression and joy;
Know my lovers and mistakes;
Know my appetite for books
Food
Lust
Rest
Life
Art;
Know the way I live,
More than I do.

To What I Pass On

My father always wanted a son,
told my mother no matter what,
my name would be Timothy Vernon Hall II, after him.

I had no say in my body or this world,
someone prayed that I would be born.
When the doctor checked the boy box on my birth certificate,
he probably told my parents "this boy will be good"
Most likely gave them the typical
male privilege schpeal.
Told them this little boy will grow into a big strong man,
Will know what he wants in life,
Will be the head of his household
The breadwinner of his relationships.
This boy will be a heart breaker,
Women will want him,

The "how to be a man" messages boy received from movies and TV
shows weren't that different.
Boy shouldn't be girl,
girl isn't boy.
Boys job is to tease and annoy girl,
girl is weaker,
boy bullies the weak,
even if they are other boys.
Boy is smart and deserving of certain rights as a man.

A man gets the job,
gets money and wealth,
gets the ladies,
He will have many of them,

Will collect and trade them like football cards
and know all their stats.
A man takes things,
Only thinks of himself,
but should be a gentleman, chivalrous
Willing to provide for a family,
The right kind,
Between a boy and a girl.

My future seed will not have a say
in their body or this world.
Their existence will be foreign to them
and I will be unfamiliar.
They will not know how to process their
reality, only what they are told they are.
They will be beautiful and complex,
innocent and untouched,
refreshing and terrifying.
I am the result of mixed messaging's from
binary world.
My future seed will know of my journey.

3/27/16
Practicing Metaphor

The sun, pretentious bastard son of an all too cocky lawyer.

The moons glare washes over the church roof,
raining on holy ground.

The earth, TV dinner to an over worked father.

The ocean floor lays to bed secrets no one wanted told.

4/2/16

Journal Entry

I remind myself she doesn't know my thoughts of need for solitude. My mouth is a concrete structure and her tongue - callus from having to fight, in all her woman - is a bulldozer. My bricked teeth are comfortable in their masculine fear and desire and want and concern and vulnerable and dependence of her. I recognize my thoughts don't always need a microphone, but I cannot treat her comfort in demolition as responsibility of her woman. There is nothing to fear in speaking other than understanding.

what is a Man

Men laugh.
They joke and frolic.
They hit and bump.
Men show emotion.
The dap is a sign of love or understanding or cool,
Men are cool.
They say things like
"Yeah bro", "That's wassup",
"Good shit", "That's tight".
These are not historic sayings,
Not a dying dialect, or language only found on ancient script or cave
walls.

I am a man.
I laugh.
I joke and frolic.
I hit and bump.
I show emotion.
My dap is a sign of respect,
It is how I show love,
Understanding,
Cool, it is how I show my cool.
I am cool.

I like my cool.
I like the way my smile can secure the space around me,
Like the way my father expresses gratitude
for my mother,
Like the way their laughter tangles them in hugs,
Like the way their love teaches me it's okay to smile.

I am a man.
It is important to me.
I must work at owning my humanity,
My flesh and intestine,
My trepidation and privilege,
My demons and potential.
I am not whole, and that is okay.
I am okay.
Being a man is okay.

Grandpa Prays

Grandpa sits annoyingly in his too old to toss recliner watching the Bengals get their butts handed to them by the Eagles. He riffs that it wasn't a fair win, the players know their own effort to make solid plays but didn't even put up a fight this time.

Grandpa scowls at the television, then attempts to get up to use the bathroom, rocking back and fourth a few times before his flat feet are able to shift his weight forward enough to stand. With resentment still staining his breath he mums an opinionated insult towards the pathetic Bengals and proceeds to do his business on the toilet.

Grandpa loves his football, feeds on the competition. He also loves prayer and God and the bible. Tells me every time we see each other how much he prays for me and my siblings. That he's thankful for his life and how he's outlived all of his younger brothers. Devoutly consistent he repeats this sentiment quite often, contrary to the other stories left in his memory.

Like his time in Vietnam serving in the Air Force. I sometimes don't know if the haze with which he speaks about this era is Dementia or PTSD. Grandpa never talks about the war, but loves his football; likes the completion and suspense. The way helmets crack and bodies tangle, how the announcers narrate plays and how footballs spiral in the air dropping in the arms of players like bombs.

Grandpa never talks about the war, but makes sure I know he prays for my siblings, and me religiously. Can't remember his pills or where he put the newspaper, but always prays for me. Iterates how grateful he his to be alive, how he's outlived all his younger brothers and is blessed to be breathing. When he returns from the bathroom he asks if the next game has started yet. I say yes and get comfortable on the couch. He says that he's proud of me and prays for my siblings everyday. That he's humbled to have outlived all his younger brothers, and grateful to be alive. Grandpa never talks about the war, but he prays a lot. Grandpa prays a lot.

4/4/16

Looking Glass

Looking glass looking glass
where will you take me?
I hope somewhere better tasting than any yesterday we've shared.
I want to feel the rush of being alive without risking tomorrow,
I cannot stay in this molasses of a heart anymore.
Can you deconstruct bliss for me?
I imagine it's that one thing I thought about doing a couple weeks
ago but was too scared to allow myself a moment of happiness.
Ya know, those decisions framed in the "what if" of my memory
perfectly positioned on the "keep me up at night" wall I stare at in
the muted darkness of my bed.
If you should find my purpose
please tell him I'm searching.
Waiting the moments my body moves intently,
my mouth speaks with courage,
and my hands do without hesitation.
There is a place I need to go that is not here.

Waiting for love or Saying goodbye

Bittersweet
goodbyes
flare
in the hearts
of a lovers
past.

They weren't
ready for
the whirlwind
of emotion
bombarding
their bodies
with ease.

Longing will
have its
time with
them;
time is a
treacherous
prison.

4/12/16

Dangerous Speech

Fear is a gun cocked and ready to volcano.
Either it will erupt,
showering metal, doubt, and destruction onto
everything in its forward,
or
it will stay cocked
muzzled, dramatic in its immature desire
to release dormant ghosts too haunting to forget.
Fear is a gun cocked.
Mouths should not resemble them.

4/14/16

The beauty in our moments

If dawn should show
pray that you will be present.
If flowers should bloom
smile their ability to heal you.
If ocean should rise and crash
love its calming lullaby.
If birds should soar
feel the winds hand under your chin
carrying worry away while upward facing.
If you should doubt
Or fear
Or concern yourself about tomorrow
Or yesterday
Or sometime
Or yet,
ground your presence in the beauty of this moment.
You are all that you need.

glances men should know

Him be dangerous.
Eyes rip through coat, shirt, flesh, her.
His stares be wolves teeth.

4/19/16

Where were you
when I needed toilet paper?
I called, you didn't respond.
My voice echoed and crashed against the bathroom walls,
uprooting tile and stained toothpaste on the mirror.
Aroma of last week's salmon stuck to the shower curtain like a Now-
And-Later left tacky in back pockets on hot summer days.
That bathroom felt like a hot summers day.
Where were you?
Could you not hear my squeal?
Did the high pitch of my cry avoid your eardrums?
I needed you,
your hands and feet
your know-how and courage,
your reach.
That room was empty,
no collateral damage to put in harms way and a debris filled
porcelain ditch with nothing to wipe my ass with.
Where were you when I needed you?
When I needed toilet paper,
when I needed something to put my shit on?

Daily Writing Routine

Bang-Bang.

Momma my shirt is wet.
I haven't spilt milk on myself since I was a child.
I am a grown man with a wet shirt,
laying on the ground.

Momma I haven't layed on the ground since I was a teenager and my
cousins n'dem used to spend summers over our house.

Momma my shirt is wet,
and I am laying on the ground,
why is it red?

Why can't I breathe?
Why are two demons on top of me?

They smell like burning flesh,
they sound like bells ringing,
they look like demons.
The ones you used to tell me about,
the ones who walk around with thorny smiles in pressed uniform,
the ones camouflaged as angels.

Momma am I dying?
Momma I think they killed me!
Momma, tell them my death will haunt and torment them until their
wings are reveals to the world as scorching bone.

Tim Hall is an educator, artist, and entrepreneur from Detroit, MI. He began playing music at the age of 10, and found poetry in college as a way to share his thoughts on paper. Tim draws inspiration from his lived experiences, charting the nuances of blackness, masculinity, and the beauties of life. He has performed in spaces all around the Midwest and Greater Boston areas, including competing in the 2016 slam poetry semi-finals for The House Slam and Lizard Lounge teams. You can find more of his work with SOUP - Society of Urban Poetry, and HipStory music label. Tim is thankful for every opportunity to share his art and connect with others.

CPSIA information can be obtained
at www.ICGtesting.com
Printed in the USA
BVOW09s0749230417
482024BV00001B/109/P